W9-DAN-526

Crestwood House

SPORTS HEADLINERS

JACKIE JOYNER-KERSEE

CARL R. GREEN

DISCARD

CRESTWOOD HOUSE

NEW YORK

MAXWELL MACMILLAN CANADA

TORONTO

MAXWELL MACMILLAN INTERNATIONAL

NEW YORK   OXFORD   SINGAPORE   SYDNEY

Photo Credits:
AP—WIDE WORLD PHOTOS: Cover, 4, 6, 16, 19, 20, 24, 28, 31, 33, 37, 38, 41, 42, 44
WILLIAM F. BEHR PHOTOS: 8, 11, 12, 15

Cover design, text design, and production: William E. Frost Associates Ltd.

Library of Congress Cataloging-in-Publication Data
Green, Carl R.
    Jackie Joyner-Kersee / by Carl R. Green. — 1st ed.
    p. cm. — (Sports headliners)
    Includes bibliographical references (p.).
    Summary: A biography of the Olympic track and field star
who has excelled in the long jump and heptathlon.
    ISBN 0-89686-838-9
    1. Joyner-Kersee, Jacqueline, 1962- —Juvenile literature.
2. Track and field athletes—United States—Biography—
Juvenile literature. 3. Women track and field athletes—
United States—Biography—Juvenile literature. [1. Joyner-
Kersee, Jacqueline, 1962- 2. Track and field athletes. Afro-
Americans—Biography.] I. Title. II. Series.
GV697.J69G74 1994
796.42'092—dc20
[B]   93-456

CRESTWOOD HOUSE
MACMILLAN PUBLISHING COMPANY
866 Third Avenue
New York, NY 10022

MAXWELL MACMILLAN CANADA, INC.
1200 Eglinton Avenue East
Suite 200
Don Mills, Ontario M3C 3N1

Macmillan Publishing Company is part of the Maxwell Communication Group of Companies.
Printed in the United States of America
First edition
10   9   8   7   6   5   4   3   2   1

Contents

Jackie Joyner-Kersee's record-setting performances have amazed her fans and other athletes.

Chapter 1

"She Was in That Zone"

In July 1986 the sports world turned its eyes toward Moscow. Athletes from around the globe were gathering there for the Goodwill Games.

The pride of the U.S. women's track team was a tall, finely muscled African American. Jackie Joyner-Kersee was entered in the **heptathlon**, the toughest event on the women's program. For two days she would compete in seven grueling events. Bob Kersee, her husband and coach, thought she was ready to break the world record.

Bob's prediction was right on target. Jackie rang up four eye-popping marks on the first day. For openers she turned in a scalding time of 12.85 seconds in the 100-meter high hurdles.

That was an American best. Then she followed up with a personal best of 6 feet 2 inches in the high jump and 48 feet 5¼ inches in the shot put. To complete the blitz, she blazed through the 200-meter sprint in 23 seconds flat. "She was in that zone where you can do exactly what you choose," Bob told reporters.

The heptathlon's complex scoring system gave Jackie 4,151 points for her day's work. That put her 50 points ahead of the previous one-day record. But Jackie could not afford to let up. A poor mark in any of the remaining events could ruin her chances.

The second day began with her favorite event, the long jump. Jackie told herself to take it easy on the first round. A relaxed 21-footer would put a thousand points in the bank. When her turn came, she hit the takeoff at full speed and soared skyward. As she landed, officials hurried forward to measure her leap. But this was no 21-foot jump. Jackie had jumped 23 feet! No **heptathlete** had ever jumped further. *Sports Illustrated* reported, "It was a jump fit for a training film."

Jackie turned next to her old nemesis, the 6-foot javelin. Today the spear sailed 163 feet 7 inches on her first throw, beating her personal best. Now only the 800-meter run remained. Bob figured that a time of 2 minutes 24.64 seconds would make Jackie the first woman to break 7,000 in the heptathlon. She exceeded that goal by 14 seconds, striding home in 2:10.02. The Russian crowd jumped to its feet and cheered.

Jackie's score of 7,148 shattered the old record by 202 points. But the skinny kid from East St. Louis, Illinois, had earned more than a gold medal. She had earned the right to be called the best all-around female athlete in history.

Jackie gets comfort and advice from her husband and coach, Bob Kersee.

At a young age, Jackie learned that all things worth having require hard work and determination.

Chapter 2

A Skinny Kid Grows Up

In East St. Louis, Illinois, the story was an old one. A young track star leaves school to marry his pregnant girlfriend. Other children follow one after another. The young parents take whatever jobs they can find. The kids wear ragged clothes and eat mayonnaise sandwiches for lunch. The entire family sleeps next to the kitchen stove during cold weather.

Alfred and Mary Joyner lived that story. Their first child was a boy named Alfred Erick. Two years later, on March 3, 1962, Mary gave birth to a daughter. Great-grandmother Joyner named the baby Jacqueline, after President John Kennedy's wife. Tiny Jackie, she predicted, would one day be "the first lady of something." Over the next few years Mary gave birth to two more girls, Angela and Debra.

East St. Louis was a dying city. Factories were closing and people were losing their jobs. Many moved away. Others turned to crime and drugs. The Joyners, however, had too much pride to let poverty drag them down. Alfred found work with the railroad, but the job often kept him away for days at a time. When he returned, he sometimes drank too much. Mary, wise and strong beyond her years, held the family together.

Mary Joyner's rules were strict. At home Jackie helped with the cooking and cleaning. At school she was expected to earn top grades. Boys were off-limits. She could start dating, Mary told her, when she was 18. Jackie knew better than to argue. As Alfred tells it, "If Mary said she wasn't going to move on something, she wasn't going to move."

The Joyners lived on Piggott Street near a liquor store and a pool hall. One day Jackie saw a man shot dead on the street. Luckily, the Mary E. Brown Community Center was located just around the corner. The center was a safe place where children could read, swim, dance and play.

When she was 9, Jackie signed up for dance lessons. Soon she and her friends were performing in a group they called the Fabulous Dolls. A year later Jackie arrived at the center one day to learn that her dance teacher had been killed. Shocked by the loss, she turned her love of quickness and motion to athletics.

Coach Nino Fennoy ran the center's track program. He still remembers the first time he met Jackie Joyner. Most of all, he says, "I can still see her head with pigtails, the little skinny legs…and the smile."

Jackie started as a quarter-miler. In her first big meet, the future star ran a well-beaten last. She shrugged off the loss and practiced harder. At a later meet, she walked away with five first-place awards. Fennoy liked her toughness. Hidden inside this skinny kid, he began to think, might be a world-class runner. At home, Jackie had to convince her mother that sports were for girls too.

As a high school student, Jackie impressed her teachers with her academic achievements, and she impressed her coaches with her athletic performances.

When she was 10, Jackie beat brother Al in a footrace. Two years later she amazed her coach by long jumping 16 feet 9 inches. Impressed by her all-around talents, Fennoy asked her to try the **pentathlon**. That meant training for five events—the 80-meter hurdles, the 800-meter run, the long jump, the high jump and the shot put.

In 1976, at age 14, Jackie and her teammates earned a trip to the National Junior Olympics. In her first big-time meet, Jackie won her age-group pentathlon. Later that year she was captivated by telecasts of the Olympic Games in Montreal, Canada. Sports, she began to realize, could be more than a hobby. Maybe she could turn her athletic talents into a ticket out of East St. Louis.

Jackie is still friendly today with her high school coach, Nino Fennoy.

A Student-Athlete Blossoms

Jackie Joyner entered Lincoln High School as a tenth grader in 1977. The school's coaches welcomed her with open arms. Anyone who could win a pentathlon was certain to be a hardworking, coachable athlete.

Jackie hit the books as hard as she hit her takeoff in the long jump. Her mother made sure of that. If her children stayed out too late, Mary went after them with a switch. Before the year was over, Jackie had earned a place on the honor roll. The high point of each school day came when she dressed for the sport in season. In the fall and winter that meant volleyball and basketball. Jackie had learned to play both sports at the Mary Brown center. Impressed by her shooting and hard-nosed defense, the basketball coach made her a starting forward.

The Lincoln Tigers were favored to win the state championship. Halfway through the play-offs, an inspired team from Centralia, Illinois, ended that dream. Jackie blamed the loss on a lack of leadership. After that, when a teammate goofed off, Jackie stepped in and tried to fix the problem. The other girls quickly learned that Jackie's all-out style won games and championships. During her last two years the Tigers went 62–2 and won that long-postponed state title. During her senior year Jackie showed the way with an average of 19.6 points a game. College basketball coaches began to drop by to watch her play.

When track season started, Jackie was greeted by a familiar face. Her old friend Nino Fennoy was in charge of the girls' track-and-field team. With Fennoy's help, Jackie emerged as the team's star. In her three years at Lincoln the girls won three state titles. As a junior, Jackie soared 20 feet 7½ inches to set a state long-jump record. Along the way she added two more national junior pentathlon titles. These heroics earned her a place on the high school **All-American teams** in basketball and track.

Friends urged Jackie to party with them, but she refused. As she said later, "It took a long time before I would even take an aspirin." After the basketball team won the state title, a man tried to slip her some money. For a poor kid in ragged shoes, the offer must have been tempting. But Jackie walked away empty-handed. "Expect nothing, ask for nothing—and do for yourself" was her motto.

Jackie wanted her brother to share in her success. When she thought Al was lazing through his workouts, she urged him to train harder. With Jackie pushing, Al soon broke 50 feet in the triple jump. That effort earned him a scholarship—and a chance years later to win Olympic gold.

Spring brought new opportunities. Invited to try out for the 1980 Olympic team, Jackie long jumped 20 feet 9¾ inches. That was the best jump of her life—but it was eighth best at the trials. Only the top three jumpers made the team. She felt better when the University of California at Los Angeles (UCLA) offered her an **athletic scholarship** in basketball.

14

Al and Jackie have always shared a close and loving brother/sister relationship.

Jackie graduated in the top 10 percent of her class that spring. Three months later she made the long trip to California. Ahead lay new challenges and adventures.

When she wasn't busy with fresh-man schoolwork or basketball, Jackie worked out with the UCLA track team.

Chapter 4

Early Days
at
UCLA

College life at UCLA was exciting—and a little scary. Jackie felt lost and lonely on the big campus. Hard work brought some relief. As a history major she had classes to attend, books to read and papers to write. On fall afternoons she reported to the basketball court.

Coach Billie Moore smiled when she saw her prize recruit. Jackie drove hard to the basket and fought for each **rebound**. Though she played out of control at times, she won a starting forward slot. In 34 games that year she averaged 9.2 points a game and shot .506. She also pulled down 158 rebounds.

In her spare time Jackie worked out with the track team. The UCLA track coaches, however, had little time for her. As a

17

nonscholarship "walk-on," Jackie was left to train on her own. Without proper coaching, her long jumping did not improve. If anything, it grew worse.

In time, her speed and power attracted one set of knowing eyes. Assistant coach Bob Kersee began to go out of his way to help her. At 26 Bob was already known as a brilliant young coach. Brilliant or not, Jackie was not sure she liked him. "I only knew him as this coach who was always screaming like a madman at his athletes," she remembers.

In January 1981 Jackie's life turned upside down. A sudden phone call sent her flying to her mother's bedside. Stricken by **meningitis**, Mary Joyner had fallen into a coma. The doctors said she would never wake again. Should they turn off the life-support system?

Alfred could not bring himself to say the word that would end Mary's life. Jackie and her brother, Al, were left to make the decision. Both knew that their mother would not want to live this way. If she could not be strong, they would have to be strong for her. After praying together, they told the doctors to turn off the life support. Mary died two hours later.

Aunt Della took charge of the household. Sad and uncertain, Jackie flew back to UCLA. Wasn't it her duty to stay home to care for her father and sisters? To her surprise, she found comfort and strength in Bob Kersee. His own mother, he remembered, had died when he was 18. Mary would have wanted her to stay in school, he insisted. Doubtful at first, Jackie slowly realized that he was right.

Trust grew as their friendship deepened. "I found that I could talk to him about anything and everything," Jackie recalls.

Bob knew about her pentathlon skills. Now he talked her into trying a new event, the heptathlon. This two-day event added the 200-meter run and the javelin throw to the pentathlon's five events. Heptathletes also ran the 100-meter hurdles instead of the 80-meter hurdles. Training for this event, experts say, is like learning seven languages at the same time.

By late spring 1981, Jackie was ready to compete in the national championships. Nervous and uncertain, Jackie fell far behind on the first day. That night, in a motel hallway, Bob worked on her long-jump technique. On the second day Jackie nailed a jump of 21 feet. It was her best mark since high school. The whirlwind finish helped her earn a third-place medal.

The comeback added to Jackie's growing confidence. Bob did his best to encourage her. She had the talent to be a champion, he said.

With good coaching and lots of practice, Jackie perfected her long jump.

Over time, the long jump became one of Jackie's favorite and strongest heptathlon events.

"This Girl's the Real Thing"

Jackie emerged as a two-sport star during her sophomore year. On the basketball court her scoring fell off slightly, but she improved her rebounding. The highlight of her track season came during the National Collegiate Athletic Association (NCAA) championships. Writers called her the country's top heptathlete after she set a new college record in the event.

Sports therapist Bob Forster was equally impressed. After running Jackie through a series of tests, he told Bob Kersee, "This girl's the real thing."

Preparing for the heptathlon increased the demands Jackie made on her body. When the stress became too great, **asthma** attacks closed her air passages. Each attack left her gasping for breath. If she gave up sports, the doctors said, she'd be fine. Jackie refused. Medication, coupled with proper rest, relieved the problem.

The asthma did not spoil Jackie's junior year. Her all-around play in basketball earned her a Most Valuable Player (MVP) award. She matched that honor with an MVP award in women's track. In June 1983 her record-setting 6,365 points nailed down a second NCAA heptathlon crown. The victory also earned her the Broderick Award as the nation's best college track athlete.

Jackie and Al traveled to Finland that summer to compete in the world championships. In a cruel twist of fate, both Joyners went down with the same injury. Al pulled a **hamstring** muscle and finished eighth in the **triple jump**. Jackie pulled her hamstring during warm-ups for the second day's events. Unable to run or jump, she had to withdraw.

Bob talked Jackie into sitting out the college basketball and track seasons in 1983-84. The 1984 Olympics were coming and he wanted her to be ready. That winter he entered her in indoor track meets. The meets gave her a chance to work on her sprinting, hurdling and long jumping. During daily practice sessions she focused on her two weakest events, the shot put and javelin. When she wasn't on the track, she was pumping iron in the weight room.

The hard work paid off at the 1984 Olympic trials. Jackie long jumped 22 feet 4¼ inches to set a new American heptathlon record. Her total of 6,520 points earned her a spot on the U.S. Olympic team. To her delight, Al also made the team.

The Olympics opened without the Communist countries that summer. Upset by the American boycott in 1980, they refused to compete at Los Angeles. Jackie was more worried about her left hamstring. Competing with the leg tightly wrapped, she ended the first day in second place.

The second day brought fresh problems. Forced to favor her right leg, Jackie fouled on her first two long jumps. Playing it safe on the final jump, she took off 1 foot behind the takeoff board. Her distance of 20 feet ½ inches was far from her best.

After six events, Jackie held first place by a slim margin. Glynis Nunn of Australia was close behind. With the gold medal waiting for the winner, Glynis jumped off to a big lead in the 800 meters. Jackie chased the flying Aussie as Al yelled at her to run faster. She finished only .33 seconds behind, but that was a few fractions too many. Glynis took the gold medal by a slim five points, 6,390 to 6,385.

Al returned to the triple jump while Jackie was accepting her silver medal. No one could top his personal best jump of 56 feet 7½ inches. One Joyner, at least, had won a gold medal. Later, Al found Jackie crying. He hugged her and told her that everything would be okay.

"I'm not crying because I lost," Jackie told him. "I'm crying because you won."

Winning the silver medal at the 1984 Olympics gave Jackie the confidence to strive for higher goals.

Chapter 6

Awards, Medals and a Gold Ring

For some athletes, winning an Olympic medal is the high point of their career. For Jackie Joyner, winning the silver served as a springboard to greater heights.

Jackie returned to college athletics in the fall of 1984. With its star forward back in the lineup, UCLA's basketball team posted a 20-10 record. Jackie led the way with 12.7 points and 9.3 rebounds a game. Those numbers earned her a berth on the All-Conference team.

The women's track season opened with Bob as the new head coach. He entered Jackie in sprints, hurdles, relays and the long jump. In her "spare time" she tested herself in the triple jump. Her leap of 43 feet 4 inches was the best by an American woman that year. Long jumping in Switzerland, she set an American record of 23 feet 9 inches.

Back in the U.S., Jackie won all seven heptathlon events at the National Sports Festival. Even so, she missed the U.S. record by 85 points. Her problems in the javelin throw, she knew, were holding her back. Her score of 6,718 did set a new college record.

It was in the summer of 1985 that coach and athlete became boyfriend and girlfriend. Jackie had dated before, but sports had always come first. Now she found herself falling in love. One night Bob took her to a Houston Astros baseball game. A ballpark may not be the most romantic place in the world, but that was where he asked her to marry him. Jackie said yes.

With track meets and a wedding crowding her schedule, Jackie took time off from classes. She and Bob were married on January 11, 1986, in Long Beach, California. Al gave Jackie away and took the wedding pictures. Afterward, the newly married couple flew to East St. Louis for a visit. Jackie wanted Bob to meet her family and see where she had grown up. After their honeymoon the happy couple decided to make their home in sunny California.

Jackie took Bob's name but kept her own as well. From that day on, she signed her name *Jackie Joyner-Kersee*. On the track Bob was merciless as ever in his demands. Jackie sometimes shoved back, and sparks would fly. At home he gave her all the tender support she needed. Because Jackie hated to cook, Bob took over most of the kitchen chores.

With her college sports career finished, Jackie joined Bob's World Class Track Club. The club gave her a place to train and entered her in meets. The Adidas shoe company gave her an **endorsement contract** for its shoes. In return, Adidas supplied her with free shoes and paid some of her living costs.

In July, Jackie set her heptathlon world record at the Good-will Games. Some track experts doubted she could do it again. Jackie proved them wrong within the month. Competing in 102-degree heat at the U.S. Olympic Festival in Houston, she raised the record to 7,161 points. This one was for the American people, she said later.

Jackie's banner year earned her a bushel of awards. The biggest was the James E. Sullivan Award, given each year to America's best amateur athlete. The runners-up in 1986 were basketball star David Robinson and football star Vinny Testaverde. Her other awards in 1986:

- The Jesse Owens Award (outstanding track-and-field athlete)
- Women's Athlete of the Year (given by *Track & Field News*)
- Sportswoman of the Year (given by U.S. Olympic Committee)

That winter Jackie graduated from UCLA with a degree in history and communications. When asked how she managed to excel in school and sports, Jackie had a ready answer. "Adversity is something I have to be willing to go up against and win," she said.

Jackie's amazing performance at the Olympic track-and-field trials earned her a spot on the 1988 U.S. Olympic team.

Chapter 7

Athletes Are People Too

At 5 feet 10 inches and 147 pounds, Jackie is all muscle and sinew. Swimmers carry about 21 percent body fat, top marathon runners about 11. Jackie's body fat is an almost invisible 6 percent. Lean does not mean bony or awkward, however. Running, jumping or throwing, she is all harmony and grace. Dressed for a night out, she puts on stylish, feminine clothes.

Coaches know that many athletes with super bodies try to make it on talent alone. Jackie has never been caught in that trap. Her workouts are intense and lengthy. She remembers the early days in East St. Louis. Medals and world records mean respect and a better life for herself and her family. Ask Jackie what her limits are, and she'll say she has none. She's the only person who can stop her, she says.

Back in the 1980s, East German athletes tried to play "**mind games**" with her. Someone would conceal her marker when she was ready to long jump. Someone else would walk into her path as she prepared for the shot put. Instead of blowing up, Jackie turned her anger into a greater will to win. "I have a lot of respect for a lot of people," she says. "But don't walk over me and don't do something bad to me, because I'll change that."

Close friends know that Jackie is "strong on the outside, soft on the inside." On the field Jackie and German star Heike Drechsler compete like tigers. Off the field the two friends relax with each other. Olympic gold medalist Valerie Brisco-Hooks remembers going through some personal problems in 1984. Jackie was "always sending me cards and letters of encouragement, like 'Val, you can do it.' She's like that," Valerie says.

Fred Thompson, an assistant coach for the 1988 Olympic team, agrees. "I don't know a person in this world who has a negative thing to say about Jackie," he says. "She's a lady. And it's not just on her lips—she goes out there and does things."

When Al Joyner married sprint star Florence Griffith in 1987, friends wondered if Jackie would be jealous. Flo-Jo, as she is known, wore flashy outfits and brought real glamour to women's track. When Flo-Jo left Bob's track club and picked Al as her coach, the whispers increased. Surely, the rumors went, this will break up the family.

Bob and Jackie would have none of that. "[Flo-Jo] was free to do what she thought best," Bob said. "We [will] not let gold medals and endorsements interfere with the family." In her direct way, Jackie added, "Remember, no matter what we say, we all love each other."

Growing up poor and black did not leave Jackie with a grudge against the world. Jackie felt that, most of all, she would like to be appreciated for what she was—a person with talents and dreams. "I always tell people, 'Don't look at me as a statue. I'm a human being, and I can talk to you.' It makes me feel good…," she adds, "that I can go and shake people's hands, let them know I'm for real."

Jackie endured many intense hours of physical training to qualify for the 1988 Olympics.

Chapter 8

Olympic Gold at Last

As the 1988 Olympics drew near, Bob cut back on Jackie's work load. Aching hamstrings and a sore **Achilles tendon** had combined with asthma to slow her down. Medication and rest controlled the asthma, but control was not a cure. During one severe attack, Bob had to drive her to the hospital for treatment.

Despite these setbacks, Bob set some high goals. She could win the Olympic heptathlon and long jump, he told Jackie. He also predicted another world record in the heptathlon. "If we don't get [the medals and the record], it won't be the coaching," he teased.

When she wasn't working out, Jackie was racing through airports. She traveled and gave talks to raise money for the new Jackie Joyner-Kersee Community Foundation. The foundation's sports and arts programs were her way of giving something back to inner-city kids. She said her major goal was to reopen the

Jackie proudly displays her well-deserved Olympic gold.

Mary E. Brown Community Center in East St. Louis. Jackie's childhood playground had closed its doors in 1982.

When Jackie wasn't giving speeches, she was breaking records. In February she set a U.S. indoor long-jump record of 23 feet ½ inches. A day later she ran the 60-meter high hurdles in 7.88 seconds. That was another indoor record. Outdoors, she equaled the U.S. record of 12.61 for the 100-meter hurdles.

Jackie and her sister-in-law put on a show at the Olympic trials. Running in a sexy bodysuit, Flo-Jo flew to a 100-meter hurdles world record of 10.49 seconds. Despite heat and a sudden rainstorm, Jackie broke her own record in the heptathlon with 7,215 points. She then long jumped 24 feet 5 inches to win that event too.

The U.S. team flew to Seoul, Korea, in September. A few days later the heptathlon opened with the 100-meter hurdles. Jackie won in a fast 12.69 seconds. Then came a near-disaster in the high jump. Jackie had trouble with her takeoff and cleared only 6 feet ¼ inches. She also strained a tendon in her knee.

With the knee taped, she managed a 51 feet 10 inch shot put. Then she lost ground with a sub-par 22.56 seconds in the 200-meter run. That night Bob Forster, the sports therapist, treated Jackie with ice, **ultrasound** and massage. She slept with a mild electric current trickling through her sore knee.

Her first long jump the next day proved that the leg would hold up. Jackie's leap of 23 feet 10¼ inches set a new heptathlon long-jump mark. Then the sore knee threw her off stride in the javelin. Instead of her usual 160 feet, Jackie had to settle for 149 feet 10 inches.

Now only the 800-meter run remained. Jackie started strongly, then seemed to falter on the second lap. Could her splendid body rise to one last challenge? Jackie answered the question by picking up speed as she turned down the stretch. Timers caught her fifth-place finish in 2:08.51. The crowd cheered as the scoreboard announced a new Olympic and world record: 7,291 points! Jackie had won her gold medal in style.

Five days later Jackie fell behind Heike Drechsler in the long jump. With only one jump to go, a second gold medal seemed out of reach. Rising to the challenge, she uncorked an Olympic record leap of 24 feet 3½ inches. Moments later Jackie mounted the victory stand to accept her second gold medal.

When the games ended, Flo-Jo and Jackie posed for photos. Flo-Jo had won three golds and a silver to go with Jackie's two gold medals. As *Sports Illustrated* noted, "Brilliance needs a nation no larger than a family to bloom."

Chapter 9

New Mountains to Climb

Jackie came home from Seoul to find that America had taken her to its heart. In St. Louis, Missouri, she was introduced as "one of the fastest running and jumping and stomping women in history." Two thousand teenagers chanted, "We love you!"

For a time it looked as if Jackie were winning every award a woman athlete could win. *The Sporting News* picked her as its 1988 Woman of the Year. Always before, the editors had picked a Man of the Year. The Women's Sports Foundation named her Amateur Athlete of the Year for the second time. *Essence* magazine called her "Super Woman" when it gave her its Essence Sports Award. Jackie promptly gave $1,000 of her award to Darlwin Carlisle, another *Essence* winner. The money was for Darlwin's education, she told the ten-year-old.

McDonald's, Seven-Up and The Gap signed Jackie to endorsement contracts. Adidas renewed her shoe contract. Writers guessed that each company was paying her $100,000 or more. In return, Jackie appeared in ads and made speaking tours for her sponsors.

The deals funneled new dollars into the Jackie Joyner-Kersee Community Foundation. As the foundation's hands-on boss, Jackie was often on the phone. After talking to a top executive, she would turn to her foundation officers. "See how easy," she would say.

Bob Kersee knew better. "Jackie doesn't understand how...powerful she is," he said. "She can get a lot accomplished with a phone call that the rest of us can't make."

Fame and power did not shield Jackie from jealous sniping. One attack came near the close of the Olympics. A Brazilian athlete accused Jackie and Flo-Jo of using steroids to build up their bodies. These accusations were echoed by other athletes as well. Both Jackie and Flo-Jo denied the charges. The Olympic Committee confirmed that their drug tests were clean.

Jackie said she was more sad than angry. "I've worked hard to get where I am today," she said. At a press conference in New York she added, "I've never thought about taking drugs, even in childhood. I see what they have done to my family." Jackie was thinking of her stepgrandfather. She was still a child when he came home high on drugs and shot her grandmother.

To give Jackie a new challenge, Bob pointed her toward the hurdles. During the indoor season she won six straight 55-meter hurdle races. When the outdoor season started, she moved up to the 400-meter hurdles. That long, demanding race would build up her endurance, Bob thought.

The spacing of the ten hurdles forced Jackie to lead with her right leg over five of them. Because she preferred to lead with her left, the switch was awkward. But what she lacked in style she made up in power. At a Los Angeles meet named in her honor,

Ill health and leg injuries could not keep Jackie from the 1992 Olympics.

timers caught her finish in 55.3 seconds. The time did not threaten any records, but it erased doubts about her hurdling.

In 1990 Jackie returned to the heptathlon. She won the Goodwill Games again, but could not break 7,000 points. Bob could see that she lacked her usual fire. To make matters worse, a pulled leg muscle ended her season early. In November a severe asthma attack turned into pneumonia.

Maybe Jackie is wearing out, track fans thought. "Are you going to retire?" writers asked.

She told them to ask her that question after the 1992 Olympics.

In Barcelona, Jackie makes her first throw during the javelin portion of the women's heptathlon event.

Chapter 10

Comeback at Barcelona

Gold medals and past glory do not guarantee a place on the Olympic team. If Jackie wanted to compete in 1992, she had to earn her trip to Spain.

Another leg injury almost ended her quest before it began. Competing at the 1991 World Championships in Tokyo, she collapsed during the 200-meter run. The painful hamstring tear did more than put her out of the meet. The injury left her with doubts about the future.

Those doubts surfaced during the Olympic trials in June 1992. Jackie had a flashback at the point in the 200 meters where the hamstring had torn. All at once she broke stride and raised her hands as if to brace for a fall. When she realized that the leg was sound, she picked up the pace again.

Jackie did her best to put the injury out of her mind. "I'm not going to defeat myself by worrying," she said. "Whatever comes, accept it."

At Barcelona polite smiles masked fierce competition in the Olympic heptathlon. Jackie started fast the first day by winning the 100-meter hurdles. Sabine Braun of Germany bounced back to beat her by 1 inch in the high jump. The shot put was next, and Jackie had a dismal day with the iron ball. Her best throw landed 4 inches behind Sabine's best.

Bob could see that Jackie was upset. Instead of making matters worse by yelling, he advised her to relax. "I told her to go out and have fun, to enjoy herself," he said later.

Jackie ended the day with a time of 23.12 seconds in the 200-meter run. Sabine ran a 24.27 and fell 127 points behind. The American's strong finish frustrated the Germans and their mind games. As Jackie prepared for each field event, Sabine's teammates had tried to break her concentration. She laughed about the Germans' antics, but Bob was not amused. "Every time they try to intimidate Jackie," he said, "it's going to cost them an Olympic medal."

Sabine paid the price in the first event of the second day. Jackie's jump of 23 feet 3½ inches earned 1,206 points and cemented her lead. After that breakthrough she cruised home in the javelin and the 800-meter run. Her score of 7,044 beat Irina Belova of the **Unified Team** by 199 points. Sabine fell to a well-beaten third.

An asthma attack left Jackie gasping for breath after the 800. When she did not return at once for her victory lap, thousands of fans chanted her name. I felt like "the baseball player who

Jackie waves to friends and fans during the 1992 Olympic medal ceremonies.

Jackie addresses a 1992 news conference prior to being
honored as one of Glamour magazine's Women of the Year.

comes back out of the dugout after hitting a home run," Jackie
said later. "I was tired, but...I had to take that victory lap and
shake hands with those people."

A few days later Jackie tried to repeat her 1988 win in the
long jump. This time she lost the title to Heike Drechsler. Jackie's
leap of 23 feet 2½ inches gave her third place and a bronze medal.
But nothing could erase Bruce Jenner's words. The 1976 decath-
lon gold medal winner had pulled her aside after the heptathlon.

"You have proved to the world that you are the greatest
athlete who ever lived, male or female," Jenner told her. "You
have done what no one has ever done."

Chapter 11

Sportswoman of the Year

Athletic records are doomed to fall. Jackie Joyner-Kersee's records are no exception. Sooner or later someone will break her world mark of 7,291 in the heptathlon. Her American records in the long jump and the 60-meter hurdles (indoors) will not stand forever. But Jackie is much more than cold type in a record book.

Watch her as she walks onstage to greet Arsenio Hall. With her flashy hairdo and stylish outfit, she could pass for a rock star. But this star walks with the lithe grace of the natural athlete. "How many hours a day do you work out?" Arsenio asks.

"Too many," Jackie says, laughing.

How many is too many? Follow her through a day's workout. How many sit-ups is that? Surely it can't be 500! How much weight is she lifting? Wait a minute, that's 220 pounds! Hey, she's been running sprints for 50 minutes now. Doesn't she ever wear out?

Jackie sometimes spends eight hours a day working out. She also goes through one hour of physical therapy each day. But she wishes she could stretch the days even further. She has talks to give to teenagers about making something of their lives. Her foundation would collapse if she stopped raising money. There are classes to take as she prepares for a career in television. Someday, she promises, she'll slow down long enough to have a baby.

In 1992 the Women's Sports Foundation named Jackie its Amateur Sportswoman of the Year for the third time. *Women's Sports & Fitness* added, "[She's] also the sportswoman of the decade, the century and the millennium."

As if to prove the point, Jackie won a second World Championship, in August 1993. It wasn't an easy win. Jackie had a fever when the heptathlon began, and Sabine Braun was in peak form. Going into the final 800-meter run, Braun led by seven points. In a do-or-die effort, the American surged past her German rival in the final 200 meters. The blazing finish—Bob called it her "knockout blow"—gave Jackie the gold medal, 6,837

Whether or not she competes in the 1996 Olympics, Jackie will be remembered as one of the best athletes, male or female, in history.

points to Braun's 6,797. What more could any athlete want?

Jackie has a ready answer. She's pointing toward the 1996 Olympic Games in Atlanta, Georgia. When reminded that she's now in her 30s, she flashes that dazzling smile.

"Nothing would be greater than to finish my career on American soil," she says. "As you get older, you see younger people ready to take your place. But that's also my motivation. It keeps my fire going to see girls coming after me."

If Jackie wins the heptathlon in 1996 at age 34, that will be a record in itself. No one that old, woman or man, has ever won a multievent medal. But gifted athletes like Jackie Joyner-Kersee are born to rewrite the record books. You can be sure that no one in the track world is betting against her.

More Good Reading About Jackie Joyner-Kersee

If you want to read more about Jackie, look for Neil Cohen's *Jackie Joyner-Kersee* (Boston: Little, Brown and Co., 1992). Cohen describes her career up to the eve of the 1988 Olympics. After that you'll have to dig for articles in magazines and newspapers.

Sports Illustrated (July 21, 1986): Kenny Moore and Craig Neff—"Our Woman in Moscow"

Ebony (October 1986): Aldore Collier—"The World's Greatest Woman Athlete"

Life (October 1988): Pat Jordan—"Wonder Woman"

Ms. (October 1988): Michele Kort—"Go, Jackie, Go"

New York Times Magazine (July 31, 1988): Joe Morgenstern—"Olympic Athlete Jackie Joyner-Kersee: Worldbeater"

Essence (August 1989): Joy Duckett Cain—"The Jackie Nobody Knows"

Jet (August 24, 1992): "Jackie Joyner-Kersee Wins Olympic Gold as World's Greatest Female Athlete Ever"

Glossary

Achilles tendon   The large band of connective tissue that extends from the heel bone to the calf muscle of the leg.

All-American team   An honorary team made up of the nation's best athletes in a particular sport. All-American teams are picked by sportswriters, coaches or sports foundations.

asthma   A chronic illness marked by labored breathing, coughing and closure of the air passages.

athletic scholarship   Financial aid given to athletes that pays the costs of attending college. In return, the athletes play sports for the college that awards the scholarship.

endorsement contract   The practice of paying athletes and entertainers to serve as spokespersons for a company's products.

hamstring   Either of two tendons found at the rear hollow of the knee. A torn hamstring is one of the most painful leg injuries an athlete can suffer.

heptathlete   A popular term for any athlete who specializes in the heptathlon.

heptathlon   A two-day, seven-event track-and-field competition that replaced the women's pentathlon at the 1984 Olympics. First day: 100-meter high hurdles, high jump, shot put and 200-meter run. Second day: long jump, javelin and 800-meter run.

meningitis   An illness that causes inflammation of the membranes that enclose the brain and spinal cord.

"mind games"   Any attempt by an athlete or coach to distract, annoy or upset an opposing athlete. Also known as "psyching-out" an opponent.

pentathlon   A five-event track-and-field competition composed of the 80-meter high hurdles, 800-meter run, long jump, high jump and shot put. Pentathlon competition was largely replaced by the heptathlon in the early 1980s.

rebound   In basketball, the act of jumping to catch a missed shot as it bounces off the rim or backboard.

triple jump   A track-and-field event in which the athlete must complete a hop, a step and a jump following the run-up and takeoff.

ultrasound   The use of sound frequencies in the range of 20,000 cycles per second to treat muscle strains and soreness.

Unified Team   The name given to any athletic team from the countries that once belonged to the Soviet Union.

INDEX